Just A Smi

Kim Whitmore

Copyright © 2018 Kim Whitmore

Dedication

This book is dedicated to Collin George Whitmore, whose smile lit up the room, whose kindness and helping hands made the world lighter and brighter for all who knew him. May you always see the world as he did, from your eyes up. Don't ever look down, look up at the beauty in the people that surround you.

I love you to the moon and back and I love you more than you know sweet boy.

When the color is gone, and the light needs to shine. There comes a time when all it takes is a smile.

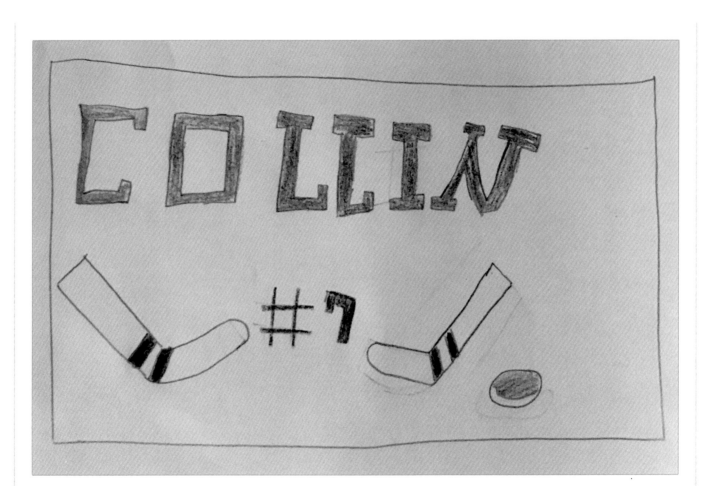

A smile to give hope and patience to those who wait.

A smile and a helping hand.

A smile and the ability to recognize those who have earned respect.

A smile to break the ice and ask for advice from those who don't realize how much they can share.

A smile and a positive word to bring out an inner strength that is often hidden.

A smile full of love and true kindness to add light and to change the world.

The End

Draw a picture of something that makes you smile.

Draw a picture of something that makes someone else smile.

List all the things that make you happy.

Write about a favorite memory.

Made in the USA
Middletown, DE
12 September 2018